'kidz-fiz-biz

physical business for kids

'kidz-fiz-biz'

physical business for kids

learning through drama, dance and song

Marlene Rattigan

Illustrator - Jennifer Rawlinson

Crown House Publishing Limited
www.crownhouse.co.uk

This revised edition published by

Crown House Publishing Ltd
Crown Buildings, Bancyfelin, Carmarthen, Wales, SA33 5ND, UK
www.crownhouse.co.uk

and

Crown House Publishing Company LLC
6 Trowbridge Drive, Suite 5, Bethel, CT 06801, USA
www.chpus.com

First published in 2004 by kidz-Fiz-Biz
PO Box 6894, East Perth, Western Australia 6892
Tel: 61 8 9325 1204
Mobile: 61 (0) 410 64 2781

British Library of Cataloguing-in-Publication Data
A catalogue entry for this book is available from the British Library.

10-digit ISBN 1845900006
13-digit ISBN 978-1845900007

LCCN 2006923066

CD masters recorded by Simon Etchell
CD replication by Media Pressing Solutions, Sutton Coldfield, West Midlands
Illustrations by Jennifer Rawlinson
Cover design and CD labels by 360id, West Perth WA, based on illustration by Jennifer Rawlinson
Scanning by Lance Rattigan
Typesetting by Marie Doherty, Cosham, Portsmouth

Printed and bound in the UK by
Cromwell Press, Trowbridge, Wiltshire

This book is dedicated to my niece, Belynda Seale,

Early Childhood Teacher Extraordinaire,

for her never-ending encouragement, support,

enthusiasm, input and above all,

belief in me and in this project.

Thank you Bim.

This book is for you, with love and gratitude.

Contents

Acknowledgements ix

About the Author...x

Rationale xi

How To Use This Book xii

All About Me – 1 1
    Introductory Lesson 2
    Complete Lesson 3
    Fingerplays –   Creeping Creeping.................................. 4
                           There Was a Little Bunny 4
                           Round and Round the Garden.................... 5
                           I Hide My Hands 5
                           Grandma's Glasses 5
    Music, Song & Rhythm –   Little Peter Rabbit 6
                           Do Your Ears Hang Low? 6
                           With My Own Two Hands 6
                           By the Light of the Moon 7
                           Street Beat 7
                           Happy Sticks 8
    Warm-up –   Come Along Now 9
    Dance & Drama –   Shake Yourself 10
                           Chopsticks 10
                           Billy Goats Gruff 11
                           Teddy Bear...11
                           Our School Rap 12
                           Running on the Spot 12
    Skills –   Roll 'em (medium-sized balls) 13
    Stretch & Relax –   Love Is Blue 14

Dinosaurs 17
    Introductory Lesson 18
    Complete Lesson 19
    Fingerplays –   Two Little Dinosaurs 20
                           Here is the Box 20
                           Five Enormous Dinosaurs........................21
                           Dinosaur Song 21
    Music, Song & Rhythm –   When Dinosaurs Roamed The Earth 22
                           Mr Sun 22
                           Music, Music, Music 23
    Warm-up –   Da Da Da Do Do Do 24
    Dance & Drama –   Dinosaur Run..25
                           Prehistoric Animal Brigade 25
                           Maggon the Dragon 25
                           When Dinosaurs Roamed The Earth 25
                           Tico Tico 26
                           Minoesjka 26
                           Trumpet Concerto in A flat Major – Allegro 27
    Skills –   Prehistoric Animal Brigade (ladder)...........28
                           Mr Sun (ladder) 28
    Stretch & Relax –   The Swan 30

The Sea 33

    Introductory Lesson 34
    Complete Lesson 35
    Fingerplays –   1, 2, 3, 4, 5, Once I Caught A Fish Alive 36
                        Over The Ocean 36
                        Five Little Seashells 37
                        Waves 37
    Music, Song & Rhythm –   Little Shell 38
                        Michael Row The Boat Ashore 38
                        Row, Row, Row Your Boat 39
                        Rolling All Around..39
    Warm-up –   Captain Cook 40
    Dance & Drama –   Baby Beluga...42
                        Seaside Song 42
                        Sailors' Hornpipe 43
                        Yellow Submarine 43
                        Sea Colours 43
    Skills –   Wheels (hoops) 44
    Stretch & Relax –   Pachelbel Canon in D with Ocean Sounds 45

Fairies and Other Fantasy Folk 47

    Introductory Lesson 48
    Complete Lesson 49
    Fingerplays –   Two Little Fairies Sitting on a Wall 50
                        Here Is The Fairy...50
                        Goblins and Fairies 51
                        I Heard a Little Fairy 51
                        A Witch and a Troll 51
    Music, Song & Rhythm –   John Russell Watkins 52
                        Goblin Song..53
    Warm-up –   Perpetuum Mobile..54
    Dance & Drama –   Dance of the Toy Flutes 55
                        Get You Moving 55
                        Puff The Magic Dragon...................................55
                        Dance of the Sugar Plum Fairy 56
                        Trepak 56
                        Minoesjka 57
    Skills –   Ice Castles Theme (scarves) 58
    Stretch & Relax –   Moonlight Sonata..59

Credits...61
Track List CD 1 65
Track List CD 2 65

Acknowledgements

Acknowledgements for their invaluable assistance go to Belynda Seale for trialing the activities and general advice; Sean Price of AMCOS for licensing advice; Lance Rattigan, Susan McCabe, Joanna Forman, Francine Giguère and Janeen Bradley for proofreading and editing; Bill Flemming from the ABC for "pulling rabbits out of hats"; Kevin Richards and Laura von Bruening from Casablanca Media and Joanne Enns from Troubadour Music for additional music and books; Stephanie Faulkner of Jackson McDonald for legal advice. Grateful thanks is also given to the many other people who have been involved in this project one way or another for their support, enthusiasm and generosity. Without your help, this book would not have been produced. Thank you all.

About the Author

Marlene Rattigan B.A., Dip. Ed. (ECS), CELTA

Marlene Rattigan is an Early Childhood teacher, a teacher of English as a Second Language, and from 1987–2000 was an AFAC accredited fitness leader. Her background is in music education. A keen interest in motor development in children led to the creation of Kidz-Fiz-Biz which she taught successfully for 13 years. Marlene conducts workshops for children, teachers and parents at schools, in the community, at festivals and conferences. This book is an extension of her Kidz-Fiz-Biz program.

Kidz-Fiz-Biz
(Physical Business for Kids)
Rationale

Kidz-Fiz-Biz is a user-friendly, comprehensive music and movement program which covers all aspects of learning – cognitive, linguistic, social/emotional, physical, and aesthetic. It will not only engender a love of moving to music but will also develop musical and listening skills through drama, dance and song. While a background in physical education or music will enhance the enjoyment of using this program, it is not a pre-requisite.

Teachers should be able to incorporate the lessons easily into their daily or weekly schedule, appreciating the links to other learning areas throughout the curriculum framework. In this way music and movement can form the basis of the yearly teaching program. It has an integrated approach, using topics to link the various learning outcomes.

Parents wishing to extend and enhance their child's development, will also benefit from the detailed notes on how to use each piece of music creatively. In this way, even those without a music background, can give their children the advantage of a vital musical education. A music and movement session incorporated into the daily life of parent and child will not only extend the parent's repertoire of games, rhymes, fingerplays and other activities to share with their child, but will also become a fun way to play with their child. Strong parent/child bonds thus formed early in life pave the way for greater mutual understanding, respect and tolerance in family problem solving later on when children become teenagers and young adults.

Stretching and relaxation is included for several reasons. It helps to develop good self-control and body awareness while improving the children's flexibility. It may also prevent injury. It is well documented that certain music can relax the mind and body while extending the imagination.

In an over-stimulated, fast-paced world, children can too easily be swept along in the rush, unable to gain the vital ability to use and develop their imaginations through lack of opportunity. My program can help to redress this balance. Children with highly developed imaginations are generally calmer and more self-reliant, able to occupy themselves rather than constantly depending on parents, other children or other external stimuli for amusement. The benefits of having these skills in adulthood are obvious.

I have loved teaching and developing Kidz-Fiz-Biz. I hope you will find it as rewarding and as much fun as I have. Enjoy!

Marlene Rattigan B.A., Dip. Ed. (Early Childhood Educ.), CELTA.

How To Use This Book

All the music has been tried and proven over many years as kids' favorites so I can guarantee its success. You can either follow the complete lessons as written, or else use them in whatever way you feel is appropriate. They are suggestions only. Feel free to add to, delete or tailor the sequence to the needs of your class. You may like to use it simply as a springboard to other things or else to gain ideas for using music creatively, whether in the classroom, daycare centre or at home. Play the music at other times during the day and observe the effect (especially when the children are painting – you may like to direct them to "paint" the music). Get involved with the dramatic play e.g. look concerned and use a quiet voice to warn children of the goblins ("Fairies and other Fantasy Folk"). Above all, have fun!

Teach "own space" at the beginning of the year or term before starting any music and movement program to develop spatial awareness and spatial memory. And, most importantly, **establish very clear rules!** (e.g. stop when the music stops; no touching others; keep a space around you, everyone goes in the same direction, listen to and follow instructions, and time-out for serious or deliberate breaches).

I advise you to **start off very slowly and simply** especially if you have a large group of children, a small space, or a group who are not used to music and movement sessions. That is the purpose of having an Introductory Lesson at the beginning of each routine. Repeat the session each day if possible, and as the children become used to what is expected of them, gradually introduce one or two more pieces as they begin to develop better self-control. **You may like to do the fingerplays, music and songs one day, and the more physical activities the next day, and so on throughout the week**. You may well find that you can squeeze in a 15–20 minute session daily whereas a 45–60 minute session may be difficult to schedule even once a week. You could even do the skills section as a mini outdoor lesson and incorporate it into an obstacle course where appropriate. If indoors, use the musical accompaniment.

The teacher/parent should model the movements but not necessarily do all the running around with the children – use this time to observe motor development and skills. Initially, the children will benefit more from the program if the adult joins in with everything.

Make sure you end each physical session, no matter how short, with some stretching and relaxation. **Stretches should never hurt** and should always be done in a slow and controlled way. It is important to slow down and stretch to relax the children otherwise they will be unsettled all day.

Overall aims: to have fun with music; *to acquire a repertoire of rhymes, songs and fingerplays; to provide an opportunity for improvisation and creative expression; to develop a sense of beat and rhythm, and musical discrimination (pitch, dynamics and tempo); to develop social skills, confidence and self-esteem; to develop listening skills and concentration; to develop co-ordination and motor skills; to develop body awareness, spatial awareness and physical fitness (aerobic and muscular endurance and flexibility); to develop an understanding of positional and directional terms.*

Kidz-Fiz-Biz

Music and Movement for Children (age 2–7 years)

All About Me – 1

Music and Movement for Children (age 2–7 years)

All About Me – 1

INTRODUCTORY LESSON

For instructions see the complete lesson that follows. If the children are inexperienced with music and movement lessons, or the teacher/parent is, then it is very wise to start off slowly and not try to be too ambitious. Having mastered this basic introductory lesson, more can be added later from the longer version. Establish clear rules (see page xii).

Equipment:	Rubber balls approximately soccer ball size – 1 per child Tapping sticks – 1 pair per child
Fingerplays:	Round and Round the Garden I Hide My Hands
Music, Song & Rhythm:	Little Peter Rabbit Do Your Ears Hang Low? Happy Sticks
Warm-up:	Come Along Now
Dance & Drama:	Shake Yourself Billy Goats Gruff Teddy Bear Running on the Spot
Skills:	Roll 'em – ball skills
Stretch & Relax:	Love Is Blue

Music and Movement for Children (age 2–7 years)

All About Me – 1

COMPLETE LESSON

Equipment:	**Rubber balls approximately soccer ball size – 1 per child** **Tapping sticks – 1 pair per child**
Fingerplays:	**Creeping Creeping** **There Was a Little Bunny** **Round and Round the Garden** **I Hide My Hands** **Grandma's Glasses**
Music, Song & Rhythm:	**Little Peter Rabbit** **Do Your Ears Hang Low?** **With My Own Two Hands** **By the Light of the Moon** **Street Beat** **Happy Sticks**
Warm-up:	**Come Along Now**
Dance & Drama:	**Shake Yourself** **Chopsticks** **Billy Goats Gruff** **Teddy Bear** **Our School Rap** **Running on the Spot**
Skills:	**Roll 'em – ball skills**
Stretch & Relax:	**Love Is Blue**

Music and Movement for Children (age 2–7)

All About Me – 1

Fingerplays: The children should be sitting in front of the teacher for this section.

Creeping Creeping

First have hands do the actions then repeat the rhyme with the feet.

Creeping, creeping, creeping comes the little cat
But bunny with his long ears hops like that!

"creeping" – fingers/toes creeping silently on the floor
"bunny" – put hands upright on head for ears
"hops" – first 2 fingers of each hand/pointed toes hopping on floor.

Outcomes: *fine-motor and gross-motor co-ordination, balance, sequential memory*

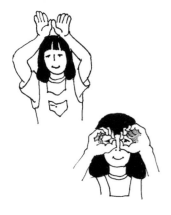

There Was a Little Bunny

Pre-teach actions.
There was a little bunny who lived in the wood (bunny ears)
He wiggled his ears as a good bunny should (wiggle bunny ears)
He hopped by a squirrel (use feet as in rhyme above)
He wiggled by a tree (body wiggles on bottom)
He hopped by a duck and he wiggled by me (feet and body again)
He stared at the squirrel (make "glasses" around eyes)
He peeked around the tree (hands over eyes, peek between fingers)
He stared at the duck but he winked at me ("stare" again and wink)

Outcomes: *fine-motor and gross-motor co-ordination, balance, sequential memory, body awareness*

Round and Round the Garden

First finger of one hand traces a circle on the palm of the other hand. First and second fingers become the "feet" walking up arm and then self tickle under the arm. Repeat, changing hands.

Round and round the garden like a teddy bear
One step, two steps, tickle him under there.

Outcomes: *fine-motor co-ordination, sequential memory*

I Hide My Hands – Marlene Rattigan

I hide my hands (put them behind your back)
I shake my hands
I give a little clap
I clap my hands
I shake my hands
I hide them in my lap
I creep my hands (fingers walking up the body)
I crawl my hands
Right up to my nose
I creep my hands
I crawl my hands
Way down to my toes

Outcomes: *fine-motor co-ordination, sequential memory, body awareness, directionality*

Grandma's Glasses

Here are grandma's glasses (pincer grip circle in front of eyes)
Here is grandma's hat (hands flat on head)
This is the way she holds her hands
And puts them in her lap. (one hand sits on the other in lap)
Here are grandad's glasses (whole hands make circles)
Here is grandad's hat (hands upwards on head – top hat)
This is the way he holds his hands
When he takes a little nap. (palms together at side of face)

Outcomes: *fine-motor co-ordination, sequential memory*

Music, Song & Rhythm: The children should be sitting in front of the teacher for this section.

Little Peter Rabbit — CD 1 track 1 (0.48)

A well-known nursery rhyme. Have children sing along. Actions to this song are quite obvious, but just in case –

Hands pointing up on head on "Peter Rabbit" for ears
Touch nose on the word "nose"
Brush hand across in front of nose to shoo the fly away
Flap arms for "fly flying away"
Hand over mouth and make a little coughing sound
Rub chest on the words "camphorated oil"

Outcomes: *sequential memory, gross-motor co-ordination, body awareness, pitch*

Do Your Ears Hang Low? — CD 1 track 2 (1.09)

Action song as per music. The children can also sing along if they know the words. See if they can roll their tongues when appropriate – lots of adults can't! (This is just a fun thing to do – it doesn't mean anything if they can or they can't as it's a genetic capability.)

Outcomes: *listening skills, gross-motor co-ordination, body awareness*

With My Own Two Hands — CD 1 track 3 (2.32)

A lovely song that children will instantly want to sing along to. Have the children rock side to side in time with the music and sing the chorus. They can put up their hands while singing the chorus.

When the song is over, ask them to recall what things were made (a tiger mask of paper mache, "ojo de dios" (a "god's eye") woven out of sticks and string, beads and baubles on a fancy chain, rhythm makers – shakers and scrapers). At craft time, the children could make some of these.

Outcomes: *sequential memory, listening skills, pitch, gross-motor co-ordination (crossing mid-line)*

By the Light of the Moon – **CD 1 track 4** (2.31)

Have the children sing the chorus ("And the wheels go round …") while rolling one forearm over the other (roly-poly arms) in time with the music (don't let them go too fast).

On "rocking horse to town" rock forwards and backwards and hold imaginary reins.

You could have them bump up and down on "with a whoopsy daisy" or simply bring the arms up in the air to simulate wheels rolling over something bumpy. Each time the chorus comes in, have them roll their arms in the other direction.

When the song is over, find out what they recall – what things happened by the light of the moon? What things do they dream about?

Outcomes: *listening skills, pitch, beat, gross-motor co-ordination, sequential memory*

Street Beat – **CD 1 track 5** (3.30)

A great exercise in listening and concentration, especially for older children. Have them slap their thighs (patsch) in time with the beat (or just listen) but when each rhythm is played, have them clap or patsch to copy the rhythm. Each one is played twice initially then the whole repertoire is gone through again. Great fun.

Make sure you **pair them up first** and have them facing their partner so that when "Miss Mew from Alabama" starts they are already in place to clap then slap their partner's hands.

Street Beat would make a great concert item for a class. Have each of the rhythm groups come out and "play" their rhythm and dress appropriately (i.e. tin can kids – have them use tin cans or similar percussive materials, have them dressed as Austrians in "lederhosen" for "Schuhplattler" etc.)

Outcomes: *beat, rhythm, listening skills, gross-motor co-ordination*

Happy Sticks – CD 1 track 6 (2.32)

A fun musical activity using tapping sticks. Model the activities so the children can follow you.

Pre-teach the various terms that may not be known –

Hammer – hit one stick on top of the other (forming a T). Change dominant hand on cue "change" (don't change hand grip).

Punch – in a horizontal plane tap the ends together, then the opposite ends together (don't change grip) on cue "change".

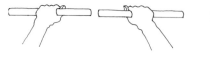 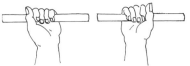

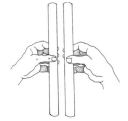

Clack – holding vertically "clack" them together avoiding catching fingers (ouch!)

At the chorus – "Happy Sticks go tapping down …" softly tap both sticks on legs 8 times then on the floor beside the legs 8 times. If you have a wooden floor, only tap on the legs.

Ensure an overhand grip about half-way down the stick. Ensure they change the dominant hand regularly e.g. if they start off with the right stick tapping on the left, have them change to left on right so both hands get equal opportunity for skill development.

Outcomes: *beat, fine-motor co-ordination, gross-motor co-ordination, hand-eye co-ordination, bi-lateral co-ordination, listening skills*

Due acknowledgement is given to Jack Capon and Rosemary Hallum for these activities.

Very young children can still enjoy this activity by tapping in time with the music. They may also enjoy some of the extension activities.

Extension activities – prior to starting, allow the children to explore the endless possibilities of these sticks, e.g. ask if they can form a letter T by placing their sticks on the ground. Also a letter V, L or X and how about an A or an H (they'll need to co-operate with a partner). Roll the sticks on the floor and up the body. Place them end to end on the floor and push the rear stick while making train noises. See if they can balance one stick on top of the other (letter T). What other things can they do? Have the children make suggestions.

Warm-up: **Remind children of the rules (see page xii). Have them all traveling in the same direction. Start off with a clockwise circle then change direction for each track. They must stop the moment the music stops.**

Come Along Now – CD 1 track 7 (1.31)

Do the actions as per the song – children need to keep time with the music – it is a basic march pace.

N.B. For "spaghetti" jeans I recommend uncooked spaghetti, i.e. stiff-legged walks, otherwise the movement is too similar to jelly and icecream.

Outcomes: *beat, gross-motor co-ordination, listening skills, interpretive movement*

Dance & Drama:

Shake Yourself – **CD 1 track 8** (1.27)

Follow the actions according to the song.

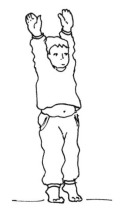   

Outcomes: *listening skills, gross-motor co-ordination, interpretive movement, body awareness*

Chopsticks – **CD 1 track 9** (2.26)

Verse – polka step. At first the children may have some difficulty in managing arms and legs in a co-ordinated and natural fashion so have them put their hands on hips while they get the legs moving in time with the music. When they can master that, then allow the arms to flow naturally. After a while, they will automatically bring the right arm forward when the left leg is in front, then the left arm forward when the right leg is in front, as with marching. In time you can add another variation of swinging both arms to the right when the left leg is in front, and swinging both arms to the left when the right leg is in front, in a rhythmical fashion.

It is waltz-time, i.e. three beats to a bar instead of the usual four, with the first beat being the strong beat. Step forward on the strong beat with right leg, bring the left leg to meet it and step off again with the right leg; follow through immediately with left leg stepping forward, bring the right leg to meet it and step off again with the left leg; and so on. It should be rhythmical and interpretive, like a dance, not forced, robotic or flat-footed. Above all, step, don't stride, as striding looks ugly and unnatural and children will tend to lose balance.

1.　　　2.　　　3.　　　4.　　　5.　　　6.

Chorus – "chopsticks" – stand and slap thighs in time with the music as though "playing chopsticks" on your thighs. The children should all recognize the music. Perhaps you could teach them how to play this on the keyboard, especially if you know the variations and accompaniments?

Outcomes: *listening skills, gross-motor co-ordination (including crossing mid-line – extension variation), rhythm*

Billy Goats Gruff – **CD 1 track 10** (2.25)

Verse – This is basically a march. Each billy-goat marches across the bridge and stops for the chorus.

Chorus – On the spot, bend knees and push hands out at chest height (in protest "don't eat me up"), bring hands back to chest (fingers still up) while straightening up. Keep in time with the music.

End – Biggest Billy Goat Gruff stands with feet apart rubbing his tummy, then the troll sings "don't eat me up" which reverts to the chorus actions.

Outcomes: *gross-motor co-ordination, interpretive movement, listening skills*

Teddy Bear – **CD 1 track 11** (1.03)

Follow actions as per song. Make sure that for "stand on your head" they get on all-fours first before they put their heads on the ground. "Go to bed" can be done standing with eyes closed and hands together against cheek, head to one side.

Outcomes: *listening skills, gross-motor co-ordination, interpretive movement*

Our School Rap – CD 1 track 12 (2.56)

This has an irresistible cha-cha rhythm. Great as a team-building exercise for your school or for a class concert – use pom-poms and streamers or other props and set up your cheerleader group.

You can let the children do their own improvised movements, or, if you want to do some kind of "cheerleader" exercise, make up a routine for them, or follow this simple pattern (or your own variation of it). If following this suggestion, ensure you **pre-teach** stepping forwards and backwards in time with the music, and grapevines (left leg side-steps left, right leg side-steps behind it, left leg side-steps left, right leg side-steps left to join it, then side-steps right, left leg steps behind it, right leg steps right, left leg steps right to join it) or side-steps (like a grapevine but eliminating the step behind).

Introduction – instrumental – pause

Chorus – "nobody does it …" 4 steps forward/4 steps back (8 times)

Grapevine – "we're dream makers …" (see picture below) (4 times each way)

Chorus – (8 times)

Musical Interlude – "doing the school yard cha cha cha" – free-form and 3 quick little steps on the spot on "cha cha cha"

Grapevine – "when you're readin' and rappin' …" (4 times each way)

Chorus – (8 times)

Interlude repeated

Outcomes: *beat, rhythm, listening skills, gross-motor co-ordination*

Running on the Spot – CD 1 track 13 (1.23)

Running on the spot, jumping, spinning – in time with the music.

Outcomes: *motor skills, vestibular stimulation, proprioception, listening skills*

Skills: *Roll 'em* – CD 1 track 14 (1.34)

Various Ball Skills

- Push ball with one foot at a time – DON'T KICK! – as in football (front of foot) and soccer (inside of foot)

- Use a tapping stick to guide the ball to the other side of the room

- Bounce and catch

- Bounce continuously (don't catch in between bounces) – have children count the number of continuous bounces – aim for 10

- Sit opposite partner with legs apart – roll to each other (make sure children push with palms; don't flick with backs of hands)

- Throw and catch to partner (control this!)

- Bounce to partner – partner catches and returns the bounce

Outcomes: *foot-eye co-ordination, hand-eye co-ordination, gross motor co-ordination, balance*

Stretch & Relax:

Love Is Blue – CD 1 **track 15** (2.36)

All stretches must be done in a slow and controlled manner. Children **must not feel pain**, just a stretching sensation.

- Firstly, have children **reach up high** with both arms, then with one arm at a time, holding each stretch for several seconds but breathing normally.

- Children kneel on the floor on hands and knees, **arching back like a cat**, holding in tummies and tucking head under towards the chest (this is called "cat stretch").

- Sit bottoms down on feet and stretch arms forward, with chest on thighs, heads down.

- Then they **lie flat down on tummies** with knees bent and **feet on bottoms**, holding feet with hands (heads must stay down on the floor to avoid stress to lower back).

- They then lie flat on tummies **propped on their elbows.**

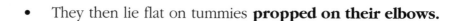

- Next have them **sit up with one leg outstretched** and the other bent with foot touching thigh; lean forward to touch toes with back straight and leg straight (it doesn't matter if they don't quite reach the toes – flexibility will improve with practice) – they mustn't overstretch – change legs and repeat on the other side.

- Put feet together close to body and push down gently on knees to stretch inside thighs.

- Next have them sit cross-legged and sitting on their hands; gently stretch head sideways so ear is reaching towards shoulder. **Shoulders must stay relaxed**. Repeat on the other side.

- Finally, allow children to lie down on their backs and stretch whole body (full body stretch) then relax with arms beside them.

- Breath in deeply and slowly through the nose and out through the mouth three times.

- Lie still and relax with eyes closed and listen to the music (you may need to replay the track – turn the volume down).

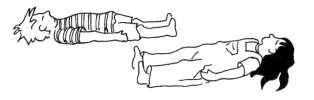

Outcomes: *flexibility, body awareness, relaxation*

Kidz-Fiz-Biz

Music and Movement for Children (age 2–7 years)

Dinosaurs

Music and Movement for Children (age 2–7)

Dinosaurs

INTRODUCTORY LESSON

For instructions see the complete lesson that follows. If children are inexperienced with music and movement lessons, or the teacher/parent is, then it is very wise to start off slowly and not try to be too ambitious. Having mastered this basic introductory lesson, more can be added later from the longer version. Establish clear rules (see page xii).

Equipment:	**Tapping sticks – 1 pair per child** **Ladder (see page 28 for dimensions)**
Fingerplays:	**Two Little Dinosaurs** **Here is the Box**
Music, Song, & Rhythm:	**Mr Sun** **Music, Music, Music**
Warm-up:	**Da Da Da Do Do Do**
Dance & Drama:	**Dinosaur Run** **Minoesjka**
Skills:	**Prehistoric Animal Brigade – ladder** **Mr Sun – ladder**
Stretch & Relax:	**The Swan**

Music and Movement for Children (age 2–7)

Dinosaurs

COMPLETE LESSON

Equipment:	**Tapping sticks – 1 pair per child** **Ladder (see page 28 for dimensions)**

Fingerplays:	**Two Little Dinosaurs** **Here is the Box** **Five Enormous Dinosaurs** **Dinosaur Song**
Music, Song, & Rhythm:	**When Dinosaurs Roamed The Earth** **Mr Sun** **Music, Music, Music**
Warm-up:	**Da Da Da Do Do Do**
Dance & Drama:	**Dinosaur Run** **Prehistoric Animal Brigade** **Maggon The Dragon** **When Dinosaurs Roamed The Earth (as action song)** **Tico Tico (Dinosaur Dance)** **Minoesjka (Dinosaurs and Fairies)** **Trumpet Concerto in A flat Major (Big and Little Dinosaurs)**
Skills:	**Prehistoric Animal Brigade – ladder** **Mr Sun – ladder**
Stretch & Relax:	**The Swan**

Music and Movement for Children (age 2–7)

Dinosaurs

Fingerplays: The children should be sitting in front of the teacher for this section.

Two Little Dinosaurs

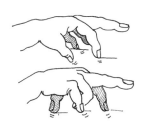

Two little dinosaurs going for a walk
"Morning" said one, "shall we have a talk?"
"Oh yes" said the other, "I do enjoy a chat"
So they walked along together with a natter natter nat.

Using all fingers of both hands, walk the fingers on the floor as you say the rhyme. The middle fingers are the neck and head of the animal so are off the floor; other fingers and thumbs are the legs.

Outcomes: *fine motor co-ordination, sequential memory*

Here is the Box

Here is the box, put on the lid.
I wonder what got inside and hid?
Oh it's a dinosaur without any doubt
Lift up the lid and let it out!

Have imaginary box in the palm of one cupped hand and put the other cupped hand over it. Gently lift the "lid" off.

Outcomes: *fine motor co-ordination, sequential memory*

Five Enormous Dinosaurs

Five enormous dinosaurs letting out a roar
One went away and then there were four.
Four enormous dinosaurs crashing down a tree
One went away and then there were three.
Three enormous dinosaurs eating tiger stew
One went away and then there were two.
Two enormous dinosaurs trying to run
One went away and then there was one.
One enormous dinosaur afraid to be a hero
He went away and then there was zero.

Have five fingers splayed to start. Hide one finger at a time as you count down. Repeat the rhyme using the other hand.

Outcomes: *fine motor co-ordination, finger discrimination, sequential memory, number concepts*

Dinosaur Song (to the tune of "I'm A Little Teapot")

I'm a mean old dinosaur	(pull a mean face)
Big and tall	(use arms to show size)
Here is my tail	(pull imaginary tail behind back)
Here is my claw	(form "claws" with hand)
When I get all hungry	(rub tummy)
I just growl	(make growling noise)
Look out kids I'm on the prowl	(teacher can try to tickle a child's tummy or each child can make menacing gestures with face and "claws")

Children can be seated or standing for this one.

Outcomes: *fine-motor co-ordination, sequential memory*

Music, Song & Rhythm: The children should be sitting in front of the teacher for this section.

When Dinosaurs Roamed The Earth – CD 1 track 16 (2.20)

Sing along to the music. Alternatively or in addition, allow the children to "free form" being the various dinosaurs – lumbering along, running fast, flying, swimming.

The children can also act out this song in the dance part of the lesson.

Outcomes: *pitch, sequential memory.*

Extension activities –

- See if the children can remember what dinosaurs were mentioned. Do they know what they look like? What size were they? How do they compare with today's animals?

- At art time, have them draw or paint them.

- Have pictures of dinosaur skeletons for the children to look at, especially the type that has the body overlay so they can see the relationship between a live animal and its skeleton.

- Bury some large bones (thoroughly cleaned and weathered and with no sharp edges) in the sand patch and have the children go on an "archaeological dig". Have a variety of paint brushes available for them to brush the bones clean after carefully digging them up. Show them pictures or a short film clip of archaeologists at work.

Mr Sun – CD 1 track 17 (1.22)

Sing along to the music and clap the beat. Simple actions can be added if you prefer e.g. form a large circle with arms (the sun), "hide" behind hands, finger action of sun shining down (like raindrops), pointing to self ("shining on me").

Outcomes: *pitch, sequential memory, beat, gross-motor co-ordination*

Extension activity –

Discuss with the children what life was like in the time of the dinosaurs. Was the sun shining on the animals? What happened to them? Why did they die?

Music, Music, Music – **CD 1 track 18** (2.22)

With tapping sticks, follow actions as per song, keeping in time with the music. Perfect for 3–4-year-olds (or younger) and a good introduction to musical instruments for all children not yet familiar with them. Ensure overhand grip about half-way down the sticks. Don't forget to change dominant hand from time to time i.e. if the child has the right-hand stick tapping on the left-hand stick, change it over to left on right.

This is also a good activity done standing so children can turn around.

Outcomes: *beat, listening skills, gross-motor co-ordination, body awareness, proprioception, bi-lateral co-ordination, awareness of positional terms*

Warm-up: Remind children of the rules (see page xii). Have them all traveling in the same direction. Start off with a clockwise circle then change direction for each track. They must stop the moment the music stops.

Da Da Da Do Do Do – CD 1 track 19 (3.10)

Introduction – 16 beats, wait (you could have the children count up to eight two times – in their heads, otherwise they'll miss the start because of the din).

Start marching. This track gives enormous opportunity for moving in all sorts of creative ways while still doing a basic march. These are just a few suggestions –

Follow the leader – march in a circle; then in a square, then in a triangle. Children aged 5 and over can cope with a figure 8 which entails weaving through a line – great for spatial awareness. Have your teacher assistant at the end of the line and do a spiral (do not join the circle but move inside the circle). When you are too squashy, have everyone turn around and move in the opposite direction. The assistant is now the leader. Hilarious fun. Older children love the responsibility of being on the end of the line and leading the group at the end.

March on heels, on outsides of feet, on toes with arms stretched up, crouched down.

March backwards (only do this if space permits), sideways (side-step), crossover sideways in front and behind then reverse direction.

Stand and do grapevines (see "Our School Rap" on page 12).

March in a circle and do various arm movements. Arms up and down to shoulder height, in and out at chest height, extend sideways at shoulder height, bend elbows so that wrists come up to chest (bicep curls).

Outcomes: *gross-motor co-ordination, balance, flexibility, spatial awareness, proprioception, listening skills.*

Dance & Drama:

Dinosaur Run – CD 1 track 20 (2.57)

Do actions as per each dinosaur (e.g. pterodactyl flies, T-Rex has short forelegs etc.), dinosaurs move slowly and stomp along; slow down when music slows, then stop. Thumb points to self ("I'm their fun"), then do 1½ turns to run in opposite direction.

Outcomes – gross-motor co-ordination, balance, listening skills, interpretive movement.

Prehistoric Animal Brigade – CD 1 track 21 (1.08)

Children do actions as per song – brontosaurus, stegosaurus, pterodactyl, mammoth. If they know the words, encourage them to sing along. Finally, they choose which dinosaur they want to be – any dinosaur, not just these ones – and stay with that movement. They must move in time with the music – it is **slow and ponderous**.

Outcomes: gross-motor co-ordination, rhythm, (pitch – if singing), listening skills, interpretive movement

Maggon The Dragon – CD 1 track 22 (1.23)

Children move quickly like a dragon making fire-breathing noises (without voice).

Outcomes: gross-motor co-ordination, interpretive movement, cardio-vascular fitness

When Dinosaurs Roamed The Earth – CD 1 track 16 (2.20)

This can be acted out here as well as being sung in the music section.

Outcomes: gross-motor co-ordination, interpretive movement, listening skills

Tico Tico – CD 1 track 23 (2.11)

Dinosaur Dance – Conga

Great mambo rhythm which the children are bound to enjoy.
Have the children in line holding on around each other's waists. This
is a very basic conga line. Make sure they all understand right and left
sides of the body. They step with the right, left, right, then on the
fourth step the left foot is tapped to the side. The same (left) foot then
starts again to step left, right, left, then the right foot taps to the side,
then starts the step pattern again. Although the music is fast and the
rhythm is mambo, there is a distinct beat which is slow enough for
them to do a conga line. Pre-teach this before adding the music. They
need to understand that it only works if everyone is doing the same
step.

Outcomes: *listening skills – beat, rhythm, gross-motor co-ordination*

Minoesjka – CD 1 track 24 (3.31)

(pronounced Minooshka – thanks Christoph)

Dinosaurs and Fairies

Divide the class into two groups – dinosaurs and fairies – and have
them on opposite sides of the room. Play a little of the music and
have them guess whether they think this is dinosaur music or fairy
music. If they can't tell, continue until the next part plays and ask the
same question. They will then be able to tell the difference. Make sure
they can **ALL** differentiate between the two distinct styles before you
start the activity. Explain to them what is required.

When the dinosaur music is playing, the dinosaurs have to come into
the middle and act out the role of dinosaurs with big, slow steps.
When the music changes, they must know their turn is over – ask
them to quickly go back to their places while the fairies come out.
Fairies have to act out their roles being delicate on tip-toes and gently
flapping their wings. Similarly they must go back to their places
immediately the music changes. The fairies don't want the dinosaurs
catching them and the dinosaurs don't want the fairies doing their fairy
magic on them.

When this routine is firmly established, stop the music and ask the dinosaurs to now be fairies and the fairies to now be dinosaurs. Resume the music. You may not have time for this role-reversal the first time you play the music, but after they have done it a couple of times, they will be ready for the challenge of role reversal.

Outcomes: listening skills – differentiating between high and low tones (pitch) and fast and slow (tempo), interpretive movement, gross-motor co-ordination

Due acknowledgement is given to Heather McLaughlin for this activity.

Trumpet Concerto in A flat Major – Allegro (Vivaldi) – CD 1 track 25 (1.50)

Big and Little Dinosaurs

This is essentially a listening exercise. As in the previous activity, allow the children to listen to the music first, then explain what is required. Slow music represents big dinosaurs taking big, slow steps. Fast music represents little dinosaurs taking little quick steps. They must change when the music changes. Prompt where necessary.

Ask the children if they recognize the instrument (trumpet) that is being played.

Outcomes: listening skills – differentiating between fast and slow music (tempo), gross-motor co-ordination, spatial awareness

Skills: Ladder Activities

Prehistoric Animal Brigade – **CD 1 track 21** (1.08)

Use this as background for the slower activities – to maintain the rhythm of the movements.

Mr Sun – **CD 1 track 17** (1.22)

Use this as background for stepping – to maintain the rhythm.

Ladder – Purchase a fold-out one or have one made to measure –

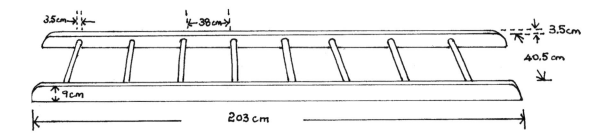

Initially the children will be trying to master these skills with the music playing quietly in the background. As they gain confidence and skills, see if they can keep in time with the music – especially the older children.

If you have a particularly large class, you may like to do this activity with a few children at a time during outdoor play to avoid children waiting too long in line, in which case you wouldn't need any background music as it would then be solely a motor skills activity.

Have children lined up. Demonstrate what is required. Only demonstrate one activity at a time. Make sure they all know which is their right leg before starting. Before changing legs, make sure they know their left leg. Have the music turned down a little.

Safety Precautions – No socks – children should have bare feet or sports shoes. Only one child on the ladder at any one time. Have an assistant to supervise the children in line while the teacher supervises the child on the ladder.

- **Walk through.** Have each child walk between the rungs using one foot after the other – they must keep this pattern consistent.

- **Gallop step.** Step over the first rung with right leg, then left leg steps over and joins it. Keep this pattern going all the way to the end with the right leg always leading. If the child makes a mistake, allow him/her to self-correct. If the child doesn't and looks like making the same mistake again, then intervene to help. Make sure every child has gone through at least twice before changing to left leg.

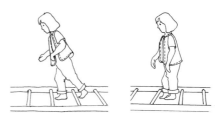

- **Dinosaur walk.** Exactly the same as a bear walk. Child walks on hands and feet on the rails, keeping bottom up. You must supervise this closely in case of falls.

- **Alternative Dinosaur walk.** Do the same as above but using only the rungs – ensure children use overhand grip.

- **Balance step.** Have the child walk on only the rungs, one rung after the other with each leg, just like the walk-through. Walk right next to the child the whole time for safety. (Don't be tempted to hold the child – be there in case the child tries to grab you.)

Outcomes: gross-motor co-ordination, laterality, balance, muscular endurance

Stretch & Relax:

The Swan – **CD 1 track 26** (3.10)

Do the same stretching routine as in "All About Me – 1" viz. –

All stretches must be done in a slow and controlled manner. Children **must not feel pain**, just a stretching sensation.

- Firstly, have children **reach up high** with both arms, then with one arm at a time, holding each stretch for several seconds but breathing normally.

- Children kneel on the floor on hands and knees, **arching back like a cat**, holding in tummies and tucking head under towards the chest (this is called "cat stretch").

- Sit bottoms down on feet and stretch arms forward, with chest on thighs, heads down.

- Then they **lie flat down on tummies** with knees bent and **feet on bottoms**, holding feet with hands (heads must stay down on the floor to avoid stress to lower back).

- They then lie flat on tummies **propped on their elbows.**

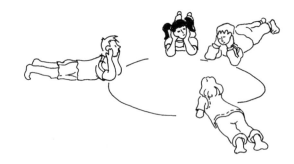

- Next have them **sit up with one leg outstretched** and the other bent with foot touching thigh; lean forward to touch toes with back straight and leg straight (it doesn't matter if they don't quite reach the toes – flexibility will improve with practice) – they mustn't overstretch – change legs and repeat on the other side.

- Put feet together close to body and push down gently on knees to stretch inside thighs.

- Next have them sit cross-legged and sitting on their hands; gently stretch head sideways so ear is reaching towards shoulder. **Shoulders must stay relaxed**. Repeat on the other side.

- Finally, allow children to lie down on their backs and stretch whole body (full body stretch) then relax with arms beside them.

- Breath in deeply and slowly through the nose and out through the mouth three times.

- Lie still and relax with eyes closed and listen to the music (you may need to replay the track – turn the volume down).

When the music finishes ask them to sit up and tell you what they were imagining while listening to the music. Who was thinking of dinosaurs sleeping? (It doesn't matter that this music is meant to conjure up images of swans on a lake; it is relaxing enough to conjure up images of any restful scene.)

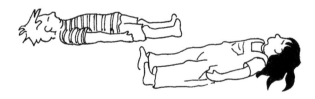

Outcomes: *flexibility, body awareness, relaxation*

Kidz-Fiz-Biz

Music and Movement for Children (age 2–7)

The Sea

Music and Movement for Children (age 2–7)

The Sea

INTRODUCTORY LESSON

For instructions see the complete lesson that follows. If the children are inexperienced with music and movement lessons, or the teacher/parent is, then it is very wise to start off slowly and not try to be too ambitious. Having mastered this basic introductory lesson, more can be added later from the longer version. Establish clear rules (see page xii).

Equipment:	One hoop per child
Fingerplay:	1, 2, 3, 4, 5, Once I Caught A Fish Alive
Music, Song & Rhythm:	Little Shell Row, Row, Row Your Boat
Warm-up:	Captain Cook
Dance & Drama:	Baby Beluga Seaside Song Sailors' Hornpipe
Skills:	Wheels – Hoops
Stretch & Relax:	Pachelbel Canon in D with Ocean Sounds

The Sea

COMPLETE LESSON

Equipment:	One hoop per child
Fingerplays:	1, 2, 3, 4, 5, Once I Caught A Fish Alive Over The Ocean Five Little Seashells Waves
Music, Song & Rhythm:	Little Shell Michael Row The Boat Ashore Row, Row, Row Your Boat Rolling All Around
Warm-up:	Captain Cook
Dance & Drama:	Baby Beluga Seaside Song Sailors' Hornpipe Yellow Submarine Sea Colours
Skills:	Wheels – Hoops
Stretch & Relax:	Pachelbel Canon in D with Ocean Sounds

Music and Movement for K-2 (age 2–7)

The Sea

Fingerplays: The children should be sitting in front of the teacher for this section.

1, 2, 3, 4, 5, Once I Caught A Fish Alive – CD 2 track 1 (0.53)

An old favorite. Have the children put all 10 fingers up in front of them, spread out. They sing along with the music while doing the actions.

When the music starts counting out the first five, have the children touch each fingertip in turn, then change hands for the next five. **They need to touch the fingers to reinforce the number concept,** otherwise it is simply a song they sing with their fingers in front of them. For younger children, pre-teach this action and have them count out the fingers before playing the song.

Do fishing action of throwing in a line in between the two sets of numbers, then action of throwing the fish back in the water.

Use pincer grip of thumb and forefinger to indicate the biting action of the fish.

Child closes the fist and raises just the little finger and wiggles it to indicate the bitten finger.

Outcomes: *fine-motor co-ordination, finger discrimination, sequential memory, pitch*

Over The Ocean

Everyone says the rhyme while doing the actions.

Over the ocean, over the sea,
Catching jellyfish for my tea.

Pre-teach the actions. This seems like such a simple activity but is surprisingly difficult for the younger ones to achieve.

They roll one forearm over the other (roly-poly arms) in a forwards direction for the first part.

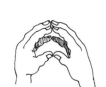

For "jellyfish" put fingertips together and push palms together and apart in a rhythmical fashion to simulate a jellyfish swimming. Repeat the rhyme rolling the forearms backwards.

Outcomes: *beat, sequential memory, fine-motor co-ordination, gross-motor co-ordination*

Five Little Seashells

Have children say the rhyme as they do the actions.

Five little seashells lying on the shore
Swish went the waves, then there were 4
4 little seashells at the edge of the sea
Swish went the waves, then there were 3
3 little seashells wondering what to do
Swish went the waves, then there were 2
2 little seashells lying in the sun
Swish went the waves, then there was 1
1 little seashell now all alone
Swish went the waves, then there was none.

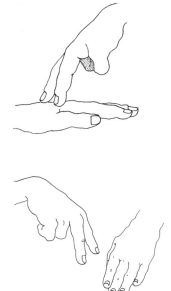

"Swish went the waves" is two hands simulating waves moving back – use backs of hands and bring them up to a "stop" position.

Children raise five fingers to start, then gradually reduce the number until only a closed fist remains.

Repeat the rhyme using the other hand to count down from five to zero.

Outcomes: *sequential memory, fine-motor co-ordination*

Waves – Marlene Rattigan

Children say the rhyme while doing the actions.

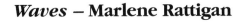

Waves roll in	(roll arms towards body)
Waves roll out	(roll arms away from body)
Waves are tumbling all about.	(roll hands over each other)
Boats are up	(palms up)
Boats are down	(palms down)
Boats are being tossed around.	(roll hands over each other)
Waves are big	(big arm gestures)
Waves are small	(cup one hand over the other)
Surfers ride them	(2 fingers of 1 hand on back of other
One and all.	hand)
Chase the waves	(1 hand is wave, 2 fingers of other hand
And run away	make the person – move hand/fingers forward/back)
Waves will catch you	(wave hand catches "person")
Any day.	

Outcomes: *sequential memory, rhythm, fine-motor co-ordination, gross-motor co-ordination, body awareness, spatial awareness, positional terms*

Music, Song & Rhythm: The children should be sitting in front of the teacher for this section.

Little Shell – CD 2 track 2 (2.18)

Sing along to the music. The children can sway slowly and gently.

Outcomes: sequential memory, pitch

Extension Activities –

This is also good to do at the end of the dance section to cool down. Have children standing and swaying with hands on hips then hands cupped in front as if carrying the shell. Make large arm movements to simulate waves. Finish with swaying and hands on hips. Children sing along.

Outcomes: gross-motor co-ordination especially crossing the midline

Michael Row The Boat Ashore – CD 2 track 3 (2.19)

Sing along to the music. Children can also paddle from side to side while singing. Alternatively, you can have them rocking forwards and backwards and doing pulling movements as if pulling oars.

Outcomes: sequential memory, pitch, gross-motor co-ordination – crossing the midline (paddling)

Row, Row, Row Your Boat

Action song. There is no accompanying music as this is so well known.

Have children in pairs seated opposite one another with **bent knees** and holding hands with monkey grip. Their legs must not be straight. Sing the song while rocking forwards and backwards in time with the beat. They are engaging postural muscles so it needs to be more than a slight movement in either direction. Having moved backwards, the partner pulls the child forwards again as he/she leans back.

The words are –

Row, row, row your boat gently down the stream

Merrily, merrily, merrily, merrily, life is but a dream. (Repeat)

Alternative second line – If you see a crocodile, don't forget to scream. (This alternative is only for a relatively controlled group otherwise you'll have the whole class screaming and losing control.)

Outcomes: *beat, pitch, sequential memory, muscular endurance, balance, gross-motor co-ordination*

Rolling All Around – **CD 2 track 4** (1.23)

Follow the actions as per song – rocking and rolling from side to side, bumping up and down. See if they can sing along.

Outcomes: *beat, gross-motor co-ordination, balance*

Warm-up: Remind children of the rules (see page xii). Have them all traveling in the same direction. Start off with a clockwise circle then change direction for each track. They must stop the moment the music stops.

Captain Cook – CD 2 track 5 (3.12)

This is a game of follow-the-leader, the teacher being the leader. Have children standing in a circle. **Pre-teach the actions**. Do the actions as they appear in the song. When the music starts, march in a circle and continue marching while doing the actions, except as indicated.

- "Captain Cook was a British sailor" – salute repeatedly.

- "sail away" – wave.

- "Captain Cook took a look" – put hand to forehead and look around **slowly. Keep marching in time**.

- "to start a colony". Slow your actions down as the music slows until you actually stop for just a moment, balancing on one foot while the heel of the other foot is touching the ground in front as though you are frozen mid-step. When the music resumes its normal tempo again, stay balanced on the same foot while the other foot toe taps behind you then steps forward into a march again. **It is essential that you pre-teach this.**

1.   2.   3.

- "maps" – draw a square in front of you using both hands.

- "sailed up the coastline" – do a paddling action on either side of your body.

- "ran aground on the Barrier Reef" – put both palms up making a double "stop" sign, while marching on the spot.

- "prepared his ship and headed home" – make a pulling action using one hand after the other as if pulling down on ropes to unfurl the sails. This is only for a few seconds as you then change your direction to indicate heading home.

- musical finale is a sailors' hornpipe. Have the children face inside the circle. Do heel jacks – hands on hips and balancing on one foot while the other taps in front with the heel then steps back in line with the balance foot. The tapping foot now takes over the balance role – shift body weight to that foot. The first foot now heel taps in front and so on. These actions must be smooth and rhythmic. When the children have mastered this relatively rhythmically, (16 beats should be enough time) then add in "roly-poly arms" which is circling the forearms around each other. After a while (another 16 beats) roll arms in the other direction. Children will often rush either the arm or the leg movements when they are put together. If you have a very young group or children with little experience or low skill levels, then do just the leg movements. Wait until they are more experienced and confident before combining them. Always set them up to succeed.

Outcomes: *listening skills, gross-motor co-ordination including balance and crossing the midline, interpretive movement, rhythm*

Dance & Drama:

Baby Beluga – CD 2 track 6 (2.24)

Slow and gentle swimming actions throughout (I suggest breaststroke as it's slow and rhythmic – more appropriate for the tone of the song) while walking in a circle.

"heaven above and the sea below" – point up then down.

"dive" – dive action.

"waves roll in/out" – roly-poly arms away from body then towards body.

"water squirting out of your spout" – hand on head then quickly up straight.

"curl up" – lift shoulders, put head to one side on hands.

"moon and stars" – point up.

Outcomes: gross-motor co-ordination, listening skills, interpretive movement

Seaside Song – CD 2 track 7 (2.14)

Appealing and easy action song.

Swim – any swimming action.

Sway – stand with legs apart and shift body weight to cross midline. Arms swing across body in unison.

Jump over "waves" forwards.

Float – stand still with chin up.

Starfish – arms out at shoulder height, standing with legs apart.

Crab crawl – sideways on hands and feet, tummies up – make a table out of your body. **(You may like to pre-teach this.)**

Swim – as at beginning.

Outcomes: gross-motor co-ordination, motor skills, body awareness, muscular endurance (crab crawl)

Sailors' Hornpipe — CD 2 track 8 (1.51)

Traditional dance which children will love as the music gets faster and faster. See the finale of **Captain Cook** for directions (page 41).

Outcomes: *listening skills, tempo, gross-motor co-ordination*

Yellow Submarine — CD 2 track 9 (1.47)

A well-known song to sing and march to.
Introduction – stand, bend knees and clap hands in time with the music.
Chorus – march and sing "we all live in a yellow submarine".
Verse – stop and bend knees again.
"And the band begins to play" – conduct the orchestra.
Chorus – march and sing again.

Outcomes: *gross-motor co-ordination, listening skills, pitch, beat*

Sea Colours — CD 2 track 10 (2.32)

Simple listening song. When the children are more familiar with the activity, have them join in with the singing.

Have children placed in 4 groups – red, blue, octopus, yellow. Initially everyone is seated. Each group stands or sits on cue.

Outcomes: *listening skills, gross-motor co-ordination, proprioception, directionality*

Skills:

Wheels – CD 2 track 11 (1.44)

Hoops

Each child has a hoop and their own space. Make sure they are not too close to each other. There are lots of activities and variations that you can do with hoops. Here are just a few. You can try one or two or all of them, depending on time and skill levels of the children.

Never overdo an activity. Stop when you feel they've had enough time and before they get bored. They will improve their skills with practice. Keep the pace going and keep it fun. When the children are positioned and ready, then play the music as quiet background music to set the mood and pace and keep you to time.

- Have each child pick up their hoop and hold it above their head with open palms facing outwards – they are standing directly underneath. On your command they drop the hoop by pulling their arms in, so they are now standing inside it. Repeat it a few times. The idea is for the hoop to drop without touching their bodies.

- Have them walk around on top of the hoop without falling off – both directions.

- Do straddle jumps all around it forwards and backwards. One foot is inside and one is outside the circle. Feet mustn't touch the hoop and **both feet must take off and land simultaneously**. Don't let one foot get in front of the other or they will naturally start gallop-ing instead of jumping. Jumping should be rhythmic. See if they can jump in time with the music. Keep it short – only about eight jumps before stopping them to rest, then repeating backwards (only if you feel they are up to this challenge and it is age appropriate).

- Standing inside the circle, jump out. Jump back in forwards, then as skill improves jump in backwards. **Two feet must be placed side by side and must take off and land simultaneously**.

- Jump in and out sideways.

- Hop in and out, forwards and backwards.

- See if they can jump over the whole hoop – do **not** suggest this if they are using very large hoops or their skill level is not up to it. (6 and 7 year olds should relish this challenge.) Remember that a jump is not a leap. Of course you can suggest a leap. **Make sure it will be safe – no slippery surfaces.**

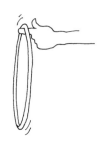

- Have children pick up their hoop and balance it on one finger.

Outcomes: *gross-motor co-ordination, bi-lateral co-ordination, laterality, directionality, body awareness, proprioception, balance, fine-motor co-ordination*

Stretch & Relax:

Pachelbel Canon in D with Ocean Sounds – CD 2 track 12 (6.40)

All stretches must be done in a slow and controlled manner. Children **must not feel pain**, just a stretching sensation.

- Firstly, have children **reach up high** with both arms, then with one arm at a time, holding each stretch for several seconds but breathing normally.

- Children kneel on the floor on hands and knees, **arching back like a cat**, holding in tummies and tucking head under towards the chest (this is called "cat stretch").

- Sit bottoms down on feet and stretch arms forward, with chest on thighs, heads down.

- Then they **lie flat down on tummies** with knees bent and **feet on bottoms**, holding feet with hands (heads must stay down on the floor to avoid stress to lower back).

- They then lie flat on tummies **propped on their elbows.**

- Next have them **sit up with one leg outstretched** and the other bent with foot touching thigh; lean forward to touch toes with back straight and leg straight (it doesn't matter if they don't quite reach the toes – flexibility will improve with practice) – they mustn't overstretch – change legs and repeat on the other side.

- Put feet together close to body and push down gently on knees to stretch inside thighs.

- Next have them sit cross-legged and sitting on their hands; gently stretch head sideways so ear is reaching towards shoulder. **Shoulders must stay relaxed**. Repeat on the other side.

- Finally, allow children to lie down on their backs and stretch whole body (full body stretch) then relax with arms beside them.

- Breath in deeply and slowly through the nose and out through the mouth three times.

- Lie still and relax with eyes closed and listen to the music (you may need to replay the track – turn the volume down).

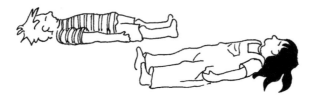

Outcomes: *flexibility, body awareness, relaxation*

This is also lovely music to play in the background while the children draw or paint. You may find them painting the seagulls and waves they can hear.

Kidz-Fiz-Biz

Music and Movement for Children (age 2–7)

Fairies and other Fantasy Folk

Music and Movement for Children (age 2–7)

Fairies and other Fantasy Folk

INTRODUCTORY LESSON

For instructions see the complete lesson that follows. If children are inexperienced with music and movement lessons, or the teacher/parent is, then it is very wise to start off slowly and not try to be too ambitious. Having mastered this basic introductory lesson, more can be added later from the longer version. Establish clear rules (see page xii).

Equipment:	**Percussion instruments** **Scarves – one per child**
Fingerplays:	**Two Little Fairies Sitting on a Wall** **Here Is The Fairy**
Music, Song, & Rhythm:	**John Russell Watkins** **Goblin Song**
Warm-up:	**Perpetuum Mobile**
Dance & Drama:	**Get You Moving** **Dance of the Sugar Plum Fairy** **Minoesjka**
Skills:	**Ice Castles Theme – scarves (fairy wings)**
Stretch & Relax:	**Moonlight Sonata**

Kidz-Fiz-Biz

Music and Movement for Children (age 2–7)

Fairies and other Fantasy Folk

COMPLETE LESSON

Equipment:	**Percussion instruments** **Scarves – one per child**
Fingerplays:	**Two Little Fairies Sitting on a Wall** **Here Is The Fairy** **Goblins and Fairies** **I Heard a Little Fairy** **A Witch and a Troll**
Music, Song, & Rhythm:	**John Russell Watkins** **Goblin Song**
Warm-up:	**Perpetuum Mobile**
Dance & Drama:	**Dance of the Toy Flutes** **Get You Moving** **Puff The Magic Dragon** **Dance of the Sugar Plum Fairy** **Trepak** **Minoesjka**
Skills:	**Ice Castles Theme – scarves (fairy wings)**
Stretch & Relax:	**Moonlight Sonata**

Music and Movement for Children (age 2–7)

Fairies and Other Fantasy Folk

Fingerplays: The children should be sitting in front of the teacher for this section.

Two Little Fairies Sitting on a Wall

A variation of Two Little Dickie-Birds.

Two little fairies sitting on a wall	(2 fists with 2 index fingers raised)
One named Peter (right finger),	(bend each index finger when named)
One named Paul (left)	
Fly away Peter, fly away Paul	(put fists behind back one at a time)
Come back Peter, come back Paul	(bring each fist to front again)

Outcomes: *fine-motor co-ordination, sequential memory, laterality, proprioception*

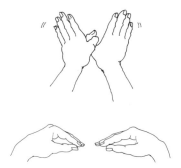

Here Is The Fairy – **Marlene Rattigan**

Here is the fairy dainty and small	(link thumbs and flap "wings")
Here is the gum tree straight and tall	(arms together straight up)
Here is kookaburra's beak shut tight	(snap thumb against closed fingers – do it with both hands)
Here is the fairy hiding out of sight.	(hide hands behind back)

Outcomes: *fine-motor co-ordination, sequential memory, proprioception*

Goblins and Fairies

Goblins are up	(thumbs up, fingers hidden)
Goblins are down	
Goblins are dancing around the town	(thumbs "dance")
Fairies are up	(fingers up, thumbs hidden)
Fairies are down	
Fairies are dancing around the town	(fingers "dance")

Outcomes: *fine-motor co-ordination, finger discrimination, sequential memory, awareness of positional terms*

I Heard a Little Fairy – Marlene Rattigan

I heard a little fairy knocking on the door	(fist "knocking")
I waited and I waited	
and she knocked some more	(use other fist)
"Please let me in", I heard her say.	(hand to ear)
But when the door was opened	(door opening action)
she flew right away.	(flying action with arms)

Outcomes: *fine-motor co-ordination, sequential memory, gross-motor co-ordination, bi-lateral co-ordination*

A Witch and a Troll – Marlene Rattigan

A witch and a troll went out one day	(two fingers of each hand)
To see what they could see.	
They met a cat along the way	(two fingers on head for cat ears)
And took him home for tea.	(make "miaow" sound)
The cat curled up on witchy's bed	(curling up arms/shoulders)
Said "This is the place for me"	
Now witchy, troll and moggy	(show fingers one at a time)
Make a family of three.	

Outcomes: *fine-motor co-ordination, sequential memory, finger discrimination, gross-motor co-ordination*

Music, Song & Rhythm: **The children should be sitting in front of the teacher for this section.**

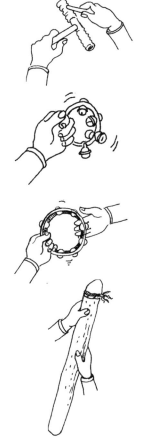

John Russell Watkins – CD 2 track 13 (2.25)

Divide children into four groups and give the children in each group the same musical instruments, for example:

(1) horses – two-tone blocks and tapping sticks

(2) ghosts – bells

(3) witches – tambourines

(4) trolls – rainmakers, drums.

These are only my suggestions for instruments – you may like to vary it depending on what instruments you have, for example ghosts or witches could have triangles substituted for bells or tambourines. **It is essential that children use both hands when playing musical instruments to employ bi-lateral integration**, for example a bell or a maraca in each hand not two in one hand while the other hand has a little rest. Don't let them bash the instruments together. They must play quietly so they can hear what is happening in the story.

If you don't have enough instruments to go around, then the children will have to take turns. Those who don't have instruments could have another job to do e.g. horses could make clicking noises with their tongues; ghosts could make "ghost" noises (good for vocal development); witches could cackle; trolls could use body patschen (slapping the body like a drum). Doing this activity initially without instruments could be a good idea if the children are inexperienced. It allows them to develop the necessary listening skills without the distraction of instruments.

Prior to playing the music, pre-teach the routine. Children listen to the song and as each protagonist is mentioned, teacher signals the children to play. All come together at the end and gradually fade away according to the music. Great for listening skills.

Outcomes: *listening skills – especially discrimination of loud and soft (dynamics), rhythm, beat, social skills*

Goblin Song – **CD 2 track 14** (2.27)

A great song for participation in a group. Very interactive and emotive. Develop an appropriate rhythmic body patschen e.g. clap hands then slap thighs, for each verse. Alternatively, you may choose to continue using the musical instruments while the verses are sung (quietly otherwise they won't hear when the chorus starts). The children **sing the chorus** getting softer at the end according to the music. On "BLAHHHH!" children open mouths wide, hands either side and shout the word. Touch body parts as stated in the song (head, hair, eyes, ears, nose, mouth). Again, as above, ensure they know the routine before putting it to music.

Outcomes: *pitch, listening skills, sequential memory, body awareness*

Warm-up: Remind children of the rules (see page xii). Have them all traveling in the same direction. Start off with a clockwise circle then change direction for each track. They must stop the moment the music stops.

Perpetuum Mobile – CD 2 track 15 (3.11)

March; fly; glide; twirl according to musical interpretation; march on tip-toes when music has a high tone; march on heels and outsides of feet when it has a low tone; big giant steps when the music is loud and booming.

Outcomes: *gross-motor co-ordination and skills development, balance, flexibility, listening skills – pitch and dynamics, body awareness, spatial awareness, interpretive movement*

Dance & Drama:

Dance of the Toy Flutes – CD 2 track 16 (2.39)

On tip-toes creeping, turning. The fairies are climbing to the top of the water-fall, but they know the goblins are about so they have to be quiet and careful, looking around as they go. When the music changes to a lighter tone the fairies are safely at the top of the waterfall so they can swim, twirl and dive all the way down to the bottom of the waterfall.

Outcomes: gross-motor co-ordination and skills development, balance, interpretive movement, listening skills – pitch

Get You Moving – CD 2 track 17 (2.42)

The fairies have to go to fairy school. This is the teacher teaching the fairies how to walk, run, crouch down low while moving, stretch up high while moving, fly, sit and especially to stop.

Outcomes: gross-motor co-ordination and skills development, flexibility, listening skills – pitch, tempo, interpretive movement

Puff The Magic Dragon – CD 2 track 18 (2.15)

March pace. You could have dragon tails or dragon wings (scarves), otherwise children can clap the beat as they march in a circle, singing the song if they can.

Outcomes: beat, listening skills, sequential memory, gross-motor co-ordination

Dance of the Sugar Plum Fairy – **CD 2 track 19** (1.51)

The naughty fairies are creeping (not on all fours) into the house through the window, along the landing and gliding down the staircase. Last night there was a big party because it's Christmas Eve. All the goodies have been left on the table and the naughty fairies are wanting to eat the scraps – yummy chocolate cake, sweets and their favorite – sugar plums! (Explain that this is the glacé fruit we get at Christmas time.) The children have to listen out for the cat and be VERY quiet while they creep around (on tip-toes) pretending to eat the goodies. They must FREEZE and listen for the cat, when the music stops.

Outcomes: *Interpretive movement, gross-motor co-ordination, listening skills – dynamics and tempo, balance, cardio-vascular fitness*

Trepak – **CD 2 track 20** (1.15)

This is a continuation of the previous story. The children now play the role of the cat chasing the fairies. It is done as a run (not on all fours). Control the speed; make sure the children change direction. If the children look like they are tiring or getting out of control, stop the music for a moment and tell them to stop and look around for the fairies. Can you hear them (hands to ears), smell them (twitch noses), feel them with your whiskers (twirl "whiskers") or your tail (waggle bottom)? Change direction again (restart the music), pretend to be going up the stairs and along the landing. A few seconds' pause is often enough to change the energy in the room and allow them to refocus and catch their breath.

Outcomes: *Interpretive movement, gross-motor co-ordination, listening skills – tempo and dynamics, cardio-vascular fitness*

Minoesjka – CD 2 track 21 (3.34)

(pronounced Minooshka – thanks Christoph)

Giants and Fairies

This is the same as in Dinosaurs (pages 26–27). The word "giants" has been substituted for dinosaurs, viz. –

Divide the class into two groups – giants and fairies – and have them on opposite sides of the room. Play a little of the music and have them guess whether they think this is giant music or fairy music. If they can't tell, continue until the next part plays and ask the same question. They will then be able to tell the difference. Make sure they can **ALL** differentiate between the two distinct styles before you start the activity. Explain to them what is required.

When the giant music is playing, the giants have to come into the middle and act out the role of giants with big, slow steps. When the music changes, they must know their turn is over – ask them to quickly go back to their places while the fairies come out. Fairies have to act out their roles being delicate on tip-toes and gently flapping their wings. Similarly they must go back to their places immediately the music changes. The fairies don't want the giants catching them and the giants don't want the fairies doing their fairy magic on them.

When this routine is firmly established, stop the music and ask the giants to now be fairies and the fairies to now be giants. Resume the music. You may not have time for this role-reversal the first time you play the music, but after they have done it a couple of times, they will be ready for the challenge of role reversal.

Outcomes: *listening skills – differentiating between high and low tones (pitch) and fast and slow (tempo), interpretive movement, gross-motor co-ordination*

Due acknowledgement is given to Heather McLaughlin for this activity.

Skills: *Ice Castles Theme* – **CD 2 track 22** (3.53)

Scarves (fairy wings)

Allow children time for self-expression, acting as fairies with fairy wings. What else can a scarf be? (superman cape, horsey tail etc.) Since this music is very slow it is also perfect for throwing and catching. At first have them throw and catch with both hands, then with one hand i.e. throw with one hand and catch with the other, then change the throwing and catching hand so both hands have turns at throwing and at catching. Catch at waist level by clutching the middle of the scarf in an overhand grip. Older children could try juggling the scarves – each child will need two or three scarves.

Outcomes: *hand-eye co-ordination, listening skills, interpretive movement, gross-motor co-ordination*

Due acknowledgement is given to Jack Capon and Rosemary Hallum for throwing and catching activities.

Extension Activities –

If you have time, before starting this activity, allow the children to explore the scarves. Depending on their age, you could ask some or all of these questions.

- What do they feel like?

- Can they name the colours (and patterns if they are not plain)?

- Have them place their scarf on the floor. What shape is it? Can they turn it into a triangle? A rectangle? Back to a square again without unfolding it?

- How many sides and corners does it have?

- Have them sit on their scarf, hold the two corners in front of them and rock back and forth singing "Row row row your boat" or "Rub-a-dub-dub Three Men in a Tub".

- Have them stand and lift one foot off the ground in front of them, tickling the raised foot with the scarf. Repeat with the other leg.

- Stand with legs slightly apart, bend the knees a little and bending forward, sway from side to side "sweeping" the floor in front of them. Repeat using the other hand to hold the scarf.

- Hold the scarf in one hand, pass it around the waist and allow the other hand to retrieve it and bring it around the front again. Reverse the direction.

Stretch & Relax:

Moonlight Sonata (Adagio from Sonata in C# Minor – Beethoven) – CD 2 track 23 (5.06)

Having done so much running around (aerobic or cardio-vascular conditioning) it is essential the children stretch appropriately to relax their bodies and minds.

- Firstly, have children lying down in a circle on their tummies, facing the centre and propped on their elbows. This is the "fairy circle" where fairy magic is discussed – use your imagination as to what the topics should be. You could ask them what they think is happening in the music – can they hear the goblins? The fairies?

- Then lie down flat, chins touching floor. Bend knees and hold ankles – gently pull until a stretch is felt; hold the stretch.

- Then do the cat stretch – on all fours with back arched up, tummies tucked in and chin tucked under. An easy way to get this is to ask them to try looking at their tummies. Sit back on haunches and stretch out upper body.

- Sit bottoms down on feet and stretch arms forward, with chest on thighs, heads down.

- Roll onto backs and hug knees on chest.

- Put arms between legs to hold ankles, and using elbows push the knees out.

- Put one foot on the floor with knee bent, hold the other outstretched leg by the toes if possible. Remember that flexibility will increase with practice. So long as the leg is straight, it doesn't matter if they can't hold the toes. Instead, with both hands around the straight leg, gently pull back till a stretch is felt behind the thigh – IT MUST NOT HURT! Repeat with the other leg.

- Stretch out whole body while lying flat then relax with arms beside you.

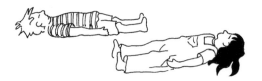

Outcomes: *flexibility, listening skills, body awareness*

Extension Activities –

Story-telling

While they are lying still and before the wake-up fairy part, you could tell them – briefly – the story of Titania. She is the fairy queen captured by the wicked goblins who have locked her in their tower. The fairies who love their queen very much, trick the goblins and rescue her. The children should be imagining what is happening in the story while they hear the music. You could ask them after they've "woken up" what happened in their story – how did the fairies rescue Titania?

Alternatively, before they lie down, ask them to listen carefully to the music and tell you afterwards what they could imagine the fairies (and other folk) doing – the music will conjure up all sorts of images for them.

The Wake-up Fairy (You may need to replay the music)

Finally, with arms by their sides, children close their eyes and listen to the music. Tell them that one person will be chosen as the "wake-up fairy" (choose someone lying perfectly still). When the "wake-up fairy" touches you, you must open your eyes and sit up without making a sound. No one, including the teacher, must speak until all children are sitting up and the "fairy" has finished. This is an extraordinary exercise in concentration and listening. Well worth it and yes, it does happen! It allows children to appreciate the value of listening and not speaking or moving. If the music finishes before the "fairy" does, it also allows them to appreciate silence. What is more, it helps them to develop some self-control.

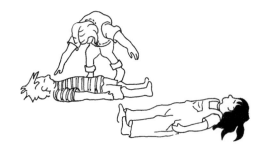

Credits

This book could not have been produced without the co-operation and assistance of the following companies and individuals who have granted me sound recording licences for the music on my compact discs. For their kind permission, I extend grateful thanks to –

AUSTRALIAN BROADCASTING CORPORATION –

From the CD Don Spencer's Australia For Kids. Sound recording made by the ABC. Produced by Allan Caswell and Don Spencer. (P) © First published 1989 by the ABC Australia.
Captain Cook – Don Spencer. Don Spencer, vocals. Bill O'Toole, Irish Whistle.

From the CD Hickory Dickory (songs from ABC Play School). Sound recording made by the ABC 1992. Produced by Val Donlon. (P) © First published 1978 Australia –
Rolling All Around – Val Donlon. Alister Smart, vocals, Warren Carr, piano.

From the CD The Best of Play School. Sound recording made by the ABC 1993. Produced by Val Donlon and Jenni MacKenzie. (P) © First published in 1993 Australia –
Teddy Bear – Traditional. John Hamblin, vocals.

From the recording Let's Have Music 1984. Sound recording made by the ABC 1984.
Prehistoric Animal Brigade – M.L. Reeve.
Maggon The Dragon – Peter Canwell (Festival).

From the CD Mambo and Other Great Dances for Kids. Produced by John Kane. (P) © Published by the ABC 2000.
Tico Tico – Traditional. Arranged John Kane/Mark Walmsley (ABC). Mark Walmsley, John Kane, David Scotland and Phil Green, music.

CASABLANCA KIDS INC. –

365 Bloor St East, Suite 1610, Toronto, Ontario, Canada M4W 3L4 (www.casablancakids.com)

From the CD Jack In The Box 1. Produced by Jack Grunsky (www.casablancakids.com). (P) © 2001 Jack Grunsky Productions. Published by Wood Rooster Music (c/o Casablanca Media Publishing Inc.), SOCAN, Canada, 2001.
With My Own Two Hands – Hans Karl (Jack) Grunsky. Jack Grunsky, vocals.
Street Beat – Hans Karl (Jack) Grunsky. Jack Grunsky, vocals.
Our School Rap – Louise Cullen, lyrics. Jack Grunsky, music, vocals.

From the CD Jack in the Box 2. Produced by Jack Grunsky (www.casablancakids.com). (P) © 2001 Jack Grunsky Productions. 383 Wellesley St. E., Toronto, Ontario, Canada M4X 1H5. Published by Wood Rooster Music (c/o Casablanca Media Publishing Inc.), SOCAN, Canada 2001.
By The Light of the Moon – Hans Karl (Jack) Grunsky. Jack Grunsky, music, vocals.

From the CD The Cat Came Back. Produced by Fred Penner (www.casablancakids.com). (P) Published by Branch Group Music Publishing (c/o Casablanca Media Publishing Inc.) Canada, 2000. © First published 1991 Canada.
John Russell Watkins – Fred Penner/Sheldon Oberman. Fred Penner, music, vocals.
Goblin Song – Fred Penner. Fred Penner, music, vocals.

From the CD Like A Flower To The Sun. Produced by Jack Grunsky (www.casablancakids.com). (P) © 2003 Jack Grunsky Productions. Manufactured under license by Casablanca Kids Inc., Canada, 2003.
Da Da Da Do Do Do – Hans Karl (Jack) Grunsky, music, vocals.

PETER COMBE –

From the CD Wash Your Face In Orange Juice. Produced by Peter Combe. (P) © Published by Peter Combe Music P/L (www.petercombe.com.au) 2001 Australia.
Shake Yourself – Peter Combe. Peter Combe, music, vocals.
Chopsticks – Peter Combe. Peter Combe, music, vocals.
Billy Goats Gruff – Peter Combe. Peter Combe, music, vocals.
Running on the Spot – Peter Combe. Peter Combe, music, vocals.

eCLASSICAL AB –

Theres Svenssons gata 10, SE-417 55, Gothenburg, Sweden (www.eclassical.com).

© **The Swan (from Carnival of the Animals)** – Camille Saint-Saens.
© **Perpetuum Mobile** – Johann Strauss II.
© **Dance of the Toy Flutes (from The Nutcracker)** – Pytor Ilyich Tchaikovsky.
© **Dance of the Sugar Plum Fairy (from The Nutcracker)** – Pytor Ilyich Tchaikovsky.
© **Trepak (from The Nutcracker)** – Pytor Ilyich Tchaikovsky.

EDUCATIONAL ACTIVITIES INC. –

1937 Grand Ave Baldwin NY 11510 USA. P O Box 87 Baldwin NY 11510 (www.edact.com) (learn@edact.com) 1-800-645-3739.

From the CD Perceptual Motor Rhythm Games by Jack Capon and Rosemary Hallum. (P) © Published by Educational Activities Inc. USA 2002. First published USA 1973 by Activity Records Inc. Music arranged and directed by Del Casher. Del Casher, guitar. Ben Di Tosti, keyboard & synthesizer. Fred Petry, percussion. Ray Pohlman, Bass.
Wheels – Public Domain.
Love Is Blue – P. Corr and A. Popp.

From the CD Motor Fitness Rhythm Games by Jack Capon and Rosemary Hallum. (P) © Published by Educational Activities Inc. USA 2002. First published USA 1981 by Activity Records Inc. Music arranged and directed by Del Casher.
Happy Sticks – Jack Capon & Rosemary Hallum. Jack Capon, vocals. Musicians, Del Casher Orchestra.
Ice Castles Theme – Marvin Hamlish & Carol Bayer Sager. Del Casher Orchestra.

THE GRAFFITI CLASSICS –

From the CD The Graffiti Classics. (P) © Produced & published by The Graffiti Classics UK (www.graffiticlassics.com) 37 Twickenham Rd Leyton Stone London UK E11 4BN.
The Sailors' Hornpipe – Traditional. Alice Pratley, violin. Ben Smith, violin. Alison Dalglish, Viola. Cathal O Duill, Double Bass.

HARI SINGH KHALSA – PACIFICLINE MUSIC (SOCAN)

From the CD Pachelbel Canon in D With Nature's Ocean Sounds. Produced by Hari Singh Khalsa (hari@smartt.com) & Gary Sill Canada 1985. (P) © 1985 Published by PacificLine Music (SOCAN).

Pachelbel Canon in D with Ocean Sounds – Pachelbel. Hari Singh Khalsa, music. Remastered, with permission, by Sharon Pendreigh, Quick Copy Audio Services Balcatta WA.

DONNA MARWICK-O'BRIEN –

4 McKinlay Ave Padbury WA 6025 Australia (dobrien@smartchat.com.au).

From the CD Kids Songs & Actalongs. (P) © Published by Donna Marwick-O'Brien Australia 1989. First published 1988.
When Dinosaurs Roamed The Earth – Donna Marwick-O'Brien. Donna Marwick-O'Brien, vocals, music.

From the CD Singalong and Action Songs. (P) © Published by Donna Marwick-O'Brien Australia 2005.
Dinosaur Run – Donna Marwick-O'Brien. Donna Marwick-O'Brien, vocals, music.

CHRISTOPH MAUBACH MUSIC AND DANCE EDUCATION –

Christoph Maubach, Orff Schulwerk Master Teacher c/- ACU 115 Victoria Parade Fitzroy Vic 3065 (C.Maubach@patrick.acu.edu.au).

From the CD Dances for Children and Other Folk. Produced by Christoph Maubach, (P) © First published 1988 Australia.
Minoesjka – Traditional. Arrangement: Christoph Maubach.

ROLAND ROBERTS –

(www.rolandsviolinpages.co.uk).

© 2006 **Trumpet Concerto in A flat Major – Allegro (Antonio Vivaldi)**. Performed and arranged by Roland Roberts.
© 2006 **Moonlight Sonata (Adagio from Sonata in C# Minor)** – Ludwig van Beethoven. Performed and arranged by Roland Roberts.

SIMON ETCHELL AND JANEY LEE GRACE –

© 2006 **Little Peter Rabbit** – Traditional. Janey Lee Grace, vocals. Simon Etchell, music.
© 2006 **Do Your Ears Hang Low?** – Traditional. Janey Lee Grace, vocals. Simon Etchell, music.
© 2006 **Come Along Now** – Traditional. Janey Lee Grace, vocals. Simon Etchell, music.
© 2006 **1, 2, 3, 4, 5, Once I Caught A Fish Alive** – Traditional. Janey Lee Grace, vocals. Simon Etchell, music.

TESSAROSE PRODUCTIONS –

P O Box 4461 Christchurch New Zealand 8015 (www.tessarose.co.nz).

From a compilation CD produced by Tessa Grigg and Brian Ringrose of Tessarose Productions 2004 New Zealand.
© **Seaside Song** – Reid/Butcher/Wright. Arrangement and vocals: Brian Ringrose. Vocals, Vicki Galloway.
© **Little Shell** – Wood/McLaughlin. Arrangement: Brian Ringrose. Vocals, Vicki Galloway.
© **Baby Beluga** – Cavoukian/Pike/Raffi. Arrangement: Brian Ringrose. Vocals, Vicki Galloway.
© **Sea Colours** – Reid/Butcher/Wright. Arrangement and vocals: Brian Ringrose.
© **Michael Row The Boat Ashore** – Traditional. Arrangement and vocals: Brian Ringrose.
© **Music, Music, Music** – B. Baum/S. Weiss. Arrangement: Brian Ringrose. Vocals, Vicki Galloway.
© **Yellow Submarine** – J. Lennon/P. McCartney. Arrangement and vocals: Brian Ringrose.
© **Roll 'em** – Brian Ringrose. Arrangement and vocals: Brian Ringrose.

TROUBADOUR MUSIC INC. (SOCAN) –

48/2190 W. Broadway Vancouver BC Canada V6K 4W3. (www.raffinews.com)

From the CD Singable Songs for the Very Young. Produced by Raffi and Ken Whiteley. (P) © Published by Troubadour Records Ltd.1996 Canada. First published 1976 Canada by Troubadour Music Inc. (SOCAN). All rights reserved.
Mr Sun – Traditional. Raffi, vocals, music.

TWO-UP MUSIC EDUCATION –

PO Box 268 East Bentleigh Victoria 3165 Australia (www.welcometomusic.net).

From the CD Rainbows, Trees and Tambourines. Produced by Susie Davies-Splitter and Jonathon Cohen. (P) © Published by Two-up Music. First published 1994 Australia.
Get You Moving – S. Davies-Splitter/P. Splitter. Susie Davies-Splitter, vocals. Susie Davies-Splitter and Phil Splitter, music.

V & H HOLDINGS PTY LTD T/A THE MUSIC FACTORY BRISBANE –

'Rose Verona' 7 Satinwood Court Bardon Qld 4065 Australia.

From the recording 22 Golden Children's Songs. (P) © 1990 Hughes Leisure Group. First published by
V & H Holdings Pty Ltd. (hhandvv@ozemail.com.au) 1990 Australia.
Puff The Magic Dragon – P. Yarrow/L. Lipton. Nicky Steel, vocals

All About Me – 1

1. Little Peter Rabbit (0.48)
2. Do Your Ears Hang Low? (1.09)
3. With My Own Two Hands (2.32)
4. By the Light of the Moon (2.31)
5. Street Beat (3.30)
6. Happy Sticks (2.32)
7. Come Along Now (1.31)
8. Shake Yourself (1.27)
9. Chopsticks (2.26)
10. Billy Goats Gruff (2.25)
11. Teddy Bear (1.03)
12. Our School Rap (2.56)
13. Running on the Spot (1.23)
14. Roll 'em (1.34)
15. Love Is Blue (2.36)

Dinosaurs

16. When Dinosaurs Roamed The Earth (2.20)
17. Mr Sun (1.22)
18. Music, Music, Music (2.22)
19. Da Da Da Do Do Do (3.10)
20. Dinosaur Run (2.57)
21. Prehistoric Animal Brigade (1.08)
22. Maggon the Dragon (1.23)
23. Tico Tico (2.11)
24. Minoesjka (3.31)
25. Trumpet Concerto in A flat Major – Allegro (Vivaldi) (1.50)
26. The Swan (3.10)

Track List CD 2 (60.35)

The Sea

1. 1, 2, 3, 4, 5, Once I Caught A Fish Alive (0.53)
2. Little Shell (2.18)
3. Michael Row the Boat Ashore (2.19)
4. Rolling All Around (1.23)
5. Captain Cook (3.12)
6. Baby Beluga (2.24)
7. Seaside Song (2.14)
8. Sailors' Hornpipe (1.51)
9. Yellow Submarine (1.47)
10. Sea Colours (2.32)
11. Wheels (1.44)
12. Pachelbel Canon in D with Ocean Sounds (6.40)

Fairies & Other Fantasy Folk

13. John Russell Watkins (2.25)
14. Goblin Song (2.27)
15. Perpetuum Mobile (3.11)
16. Dance of the Toy Flutes (2.39)
17. Get You Moving (2.42)
18. Puff The Magic Dragon (2.15)
19. Dance of the Sugar Plum Fairy (1.51)
20. Trepak (1.15)
21. Minoesjka (3.34)
22. Ice Castles Theme (3.53)
23. Moonlight Sonata (5.06)